It Doesn't Come Easy Being a Teenage Girl

By Aria M. Bryant

Edited by Anthony M. McDonald, Sr. for The RISEN Foundation (USA) & Nia'fidahli

It Doesn't Come Easy Being a Teenager by Aria M. Bryant
Edited by: Anthony M. McDonald, Sr. for The RISEN
Foundation (USA) & Nia'fidahli

Cover Designed by Aja La'Starr for The RISEN Foundation
Aria M. Bryant for the RISEN Publishing Camp 4 Kids

Cover Photo by Aja La'Starr

First Printing: July 2011

Manufactured & Printed in the United States of America

Genre: Juvenile Non-Fiction, Mental Health, Substance
Abuse

ISBN: 978-0-9838370-2-2

Published by:
The RISEN Foundation/AS&J Publishing Group
St. Louis, MO

www.therisenfoundation.org
Email: info@therisenfoundation.org

the
Risen foundation
"inspiration delivered"

AS & J
PUBLISHING GROUP

SAINT LOUIS   MISSOURI

Dedication:

To my mom and dad and my friends and Kayla, AJ and Shandon.

TABLE OF CONTENTS

Introduction

Some kids say, "I can't wait until I get grown," or "I wish that I was a teenager" but, in my opinion, I believe that a child should stay in a child's place. A lot of times, we as young folks try so hard to rush to get grown; we can be mean and angry and do things that are way before our time. I enjoy my youth; unlike some young folks, I like to smile, laugh and act silly all day every day. My friend says it's, "because you're Aria," and I say, "Yea, I am my own me in my own way <3, so allow me to share my views on being a teenage girl in today's world."

Chapter 1: Education

Yea, we know that we have to get good grades, especially in high school; scoring high on the SATS or ACTS could get you a full ride to college. We also know when we get our report cards our parents expect for them to be good. Some of you might wonder, "Omg why she/he keep bothering about my grades she/he tell me all the time I know". The reason is, they want you to get far in life and for that to happen you need an education (you're going to read that a lot ☺).

My friend A.J is all in about getting a good education. His mom doesn't play and he likes basketball so he probably wants to do that when he gets older. He be having me hollering in $5^{th\ hour}$ and yes we get good grades. He took a college course at a community college.

A.J, my lil sister Kayla, Shandon and I always sit at the same table in our 5th hour science class. When we have to take a test that's when we know to stop playing (our parents don't play :o). Sometimes when we have to do class work we get off track. Half of the time when we have to do the work one of us is focused while the other three are talking,

so we just copy off the person that did the work.

I came home from school one day my mammy (mom) called me and I thought I was in trouble, but she was smiling. She said "I am so proud of you. For the first time ARIA BRYANT!!!!! Got an A and all high B's".

Report Card

I usually get just one C in something. Instead of saying proud she used some big word (she extra lol). When she told me I was just smiling and snickering.

Ok enough of my stories education is very important, so it can be easy for you to be successful and get a good job. Most people want to be a pediatrician or a lawyer. You'll know later which one I'm GOING to be not WANT to be (confidence)!!!

A lawyer and pediatrician make a lot of money cha-ching $$$$$$$!!

Omg: oh my god
<3: heart

I would make it Rain* (throws partier) in my house when Im rich. The Smell of money.

That's a lot of school years to be a pediatrician. You have to work real hard to get that money. When you go to college you have to focus. You can party………..

But not that much!!!!!!!!!!!!!!

Kayla Jordan (my lil sis.): she has ADD it's hard for her to work without getting distracted. Sometimes I got to put her in check l2h. She like to…………

- *Ice skate*
- *Play soccer (as clumsy she is she should have a good balance at least)*
- *Play the flute*
- *Play basketball*

She is 13 and loves me hehe {sometimes}. She goes to my school, in my grade {7th going to 8th}

Kayla is crazy, funny, can sing {like me} and has long pretty hair☺.

Shandon Boone: Shandon is funny and got some of his own sayings. He's short, but muscular, low cut with waves and loves basketball like A.J. He told A.J and me a story a long time ago in elementary. It was about how in 3rd or 4th grade when we're in PE and we would play around the world (basketball game). He said I always won I was surprised I didn't remember. Shandon said "I would get so mad" and I laughed I never thought he was mad when I would win. A.J just said "are you serious? Wow." So since then A.J said when he sees me in gym he's going to get me up and play basketball. Did he do it? NO!! Shandon loves chez-its and Oreos. We was on the phone he was like talking to his self he said "I want my Oreos?" I said "I took them" he looked under the pillow and they weren't there. I was just playing though. Another time he asked "where is my remote?" I said "look under your couch" he looked and found it. He was so confused he said "how did you know where it was? Are you in my house?" I was rolling. Ever since that happened I mess with him doing stuff like that.

Anthony Smith Jr. (A.J): I don't know where to start. Ok A.J is the funniest person you will meet. He can make you lose your breath from laughing so hard that's how funny he is. We were watching the Cosby show in class and it was this boy cockroach (Theo's friend) and he was talking weird. Some people in the class said "A.J". We said that because he acts like him and can talk like him. Me and him always talk on the phone after school he won't call no-one back besides his girlfriend (my booski) jayla. He gets mad when she gives me a hug and *especially in front of him. The two main things A.J is known for to have at school are……*

❖   *CARMEX*
❖   *BABY LOTION*

Anytime someone ask me or someone ask someone else for some lotion and I or that person don't have known we would say "ask A.J". He hates when I dig my finger in his Carmex to get some I do that on purpose too. If it's lost he would have a whole fit. One day I took it home we was on the phone and he was looking for it and I told him "I got it" so he got mad hehe. AJ is my bestie brother more of a bestie. I already got a brother and we act like real brother and sister every one knows. I'm the youngest so I act like a baby around him because I never had a brother.

AJ's sayings but it's our insider kind of lol:

- *You're not the boom.com*
- *Shut it down*
- *Toddles*
- *Salute*
- *Your not hot*
- *I'm sick of this*
- *I don't know nothing about nothing*
- *Get off my phone/line*
- *Fruit loop!*

Chapter 2: Substance abuse

Every school, at least every school in 5th grade should of did dare. Dare is when an officer around your school comes in one day or however many days during the week and talk about NOT DOING DRUGS OR VIOLENCE! You really shouldn't smoke, smoke marijuana, cocaine, do ecstasy, be on crack or do heroin. Some of my friends well not friends for real I just know them for a long time and talk to them. I try to tell not to be doing that. When they be talking about how they got high and stuff I be looking confused because why yall doing that they to extra. They think and try to act grown that stuff get on my nerves. I care about them (in a way) and that stuff not cute come on now. They messing up their future I guaranty (well believe) they going to get addicted and do it in high school and get caught. That's going to ruin their future. All of that is going to catch up to them. Doing drugs can end them in jail and stop them from getting an education. A job maybe even life man. Ohh noo.

• Marijuana: marijuana such as cannabis is green, brown, gray mixture of dried shredded leaves, stems, seeds and flowers of the hemp plant. You may hear marijuana called "pot" on the streets. There's over 200 slang terms for marijuana. Smoking marijuana causes some changes in the brain. These changes may put a person at risk becoming addicted.

• Cigarette: when teenagers smoke a cigarette it makes them more vulnerable to drug addition and mental illness. This is sad to know and nasty about what is

and how many things are in a cigarette.
There are 13 things in a cigarette.

- *Butane: lighter fluid*

- *Acetic acid: vinegar*

- *Methane: sewer gas (dirty)*

- *Arsenic: POISON! (are you serious?)*

- *Carbon monoxide*

- *Methanol: rocket fuel (unn)*

- *Paint*

- *Ammonia: toilet cleaner (dirty)*

- *Nicotine: insecticide*

- *Toluene: industrial solvent*

- *Hexamine: barbecue lighter (unn)*

- *Stearic acid: candle wax (disgusting)*

- *Calcium: batteries (disgusting)*

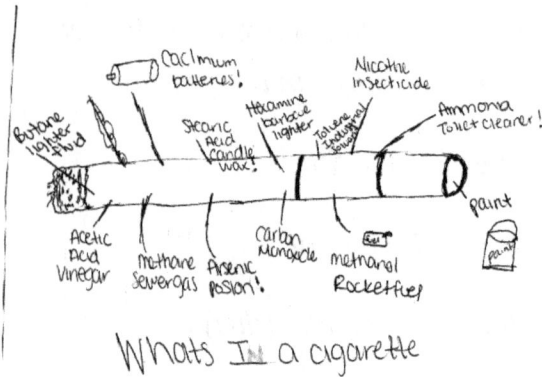

Calcium batteries!

Nicotine Insecticide

Butane lighter fluid

Stearic Acid candle wax!

Hexamine barbcue lighter

Toulene Industrial solvent

Ammonia Toilet cleaner!

paint

Acetic Acid Vinegar

methane sewergas

Arsenic posion!

Carbon Monoxide

methanol Rocketfuel

Whatts In a cigarette

Shameful!!

SHAMEFUL THAT'S JUST NASTY NO WONDER WHY YOU CAN'T GET LUNG CANCER. YOU INHALING ALL THAT.

- *5Cocaine: a highly addictive central nervous system stimulant extracted from the leaves of the coca plant. It's a crystalline tropane alkaloid that is obtained from the leaves of the coca plant.*

Cocaine can also make you want to commit suicide (YIKES!!) by depression. I think men do cocaine more than woman since the rate of suicide is higher in men than women.

• Heroine: a highly addictive analgesic drug. A naturally occurring substance extracted from the seed pod of certain varieties of poppy plants. It's solid as a white or brownish powder.

Street heroine can be cut with other poison.

- Ecstasy: MDMA is known for ecstasy. It's an illegal drug that acts as both a stimulant energizing effect. It's taken orally, usually in a tablet and last 3 to 6 hrs. Danity Kane (all girl singing group) have a song "ecstasy" if you listen t the words they're explaining what it means. Ecstasy basically means "a sex pill." It's bad for what it can do to your brain. Serotonin (neurotransmitter) plays an important role in the regulation of your mood, sleep, pain, emotion, appetite and other behaviors.

- Crack: crack is cocaine that has been processed so it can be smoked. Looks like small shavings of soap but has a hard and soft texture. It's also the street name given to the freebase form of cocaine. Crack is also highly addictive *and powerful that is derived from powdered cocaine. Crack users may experience respiratory problems, coughing, shortness of breathing, lung trauma and bleeding.*

Crack cocaine IS ILLEGAL there is 35 freakin street names for crack cocaine!!

• 24-7	• Hall
• Bad rock	• Hard ball
• Beat	• Hard rock
• Candy	• Scrabble
• Chemical	• Tornado
• Cloud	• Hot cakes
• Cookies	• Ice cubes
• Crumbs	• Jelly beans

Crunch and munch	Nuggets
Devil drug	Paste
Dice	Sleet
Electric kool-aid	Troop
Fat bags	Piece
French fries	Prime time
Glo	Product
Gravel	Raw
Grit	Rocks(s)

Chapter 3: Mental health

Some kids have mental health ☹ problems. They could have ADD, ADHD, bipolar, dyslexia, and Down syndrome. When I was little that's when they showed kids being in St. Jude on TV. I would always cry because I couldn't imagine or take a breath going through what they have/had to go through. It's so sad. Especially when I see babies in there now that's just making me cry a river.

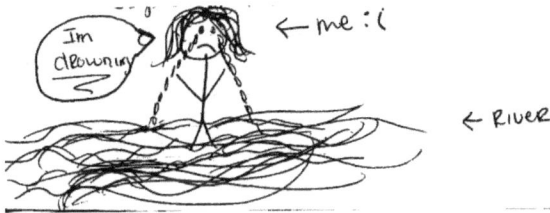

Some of them were suffering from physical afflictions and others from mental ones.

I knew from that moment I always wanted to raise money to help them.

Even better be a pediatrician to have that as my JOB DAILY. I want kids to be better and not be in that position it seems like it's quite a struggle. I also want to be a pediatrician when I started babysitting my two baby cousins 2 and 4. If you watch America's makeover home edition it starts with a sad story I always cry. Some celebrities go on there to help build the people's new house. On a few episodes they had shown families that experienced various mental health challenges. I would love to help by volunteering to make someone's life

better that faces such difficulties. I believe through helping others everything will get better for everyone. They just got to pray and sing/say to there selves:

Imagine Me (Kirk Franklin)

"It's gone gone gone all gone gone gone gone all gone"

My play director told me I could spend a day with some kids from the children's hospital. I can't wait. I might cry by being happy and sad. When I see kids that are disabled or have a disorder and feel that they're not important, loved, can't be anything or low steam they should sing/say

I believe (Yolanda Adams)

I believe I can I believe I will I believe my hopes and dreams are real. I believe Ill stand I believe ill dance I believe ill grow real soon and that is why I do believe.

ADD: (attention defect disorder) a psychological term applied to anyone who meets the DSM IV diagnostic criteria. Here is an example of someone having DSM.

Ryan: 7 yr old boy that has an IQ of 120. He has a major behavior problem in school. Constantly talks when not supposed to, gets into fights and refuses to do school work. When he doesn't get his way he throws a temper tantrum. He lies on other kids and telling on them to the teachers. He isn't fidgety just like to run and chase balls. Ryan has a fatty acid deficiency which exacerbates his negative behavior.

ADD with hyper activity

❖ Fidgety

❖ Can't stay seated

❖ Runs or climbs excessively

❖ Has difficulties being quiet

❖ Talks a lot

❖ Blurts out answers

❖ Not patient

❖ Interrupt people when talking

ADHD: (attention defect hyper activity disorder) it changes the way they/you act, think or feel. Children are overactive and inattentive at times. ADHD kids can be disruptive. If your hyper a lot or not able to stand still when you talk (ME) may have it. Unable to concentrate, moves around, poor grades and *disruptive at school. I don't have all of that.*

Bipolar: you can be happy then sad; mad then nice. It's like which one is it. Those are known for mood swings. It's a brain disorder that cause unusual shifts.

- *The ninth leading cause of years lost to death*

- *Individuals that's bipolar commit suicide*

- *People that are bipolar are at risk suffering from substance abuse*

Dyslexia: a difficulty to read, write and spell. If you "George Lopez" the boy that plays "max" had dyslexia and that's when I learned what it is. Annabelle Avery that stars in "shake it up" really has dyslexia. She played a part in an episode that deals with her dyslexia.

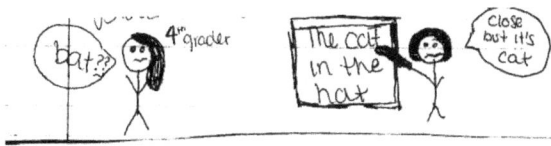

Cancer: disease caused by uncontrolled abnormal cells in a part of the body. It can be treated and cared. "My sisters' keeper" is based on a true story. A girl that played in the movie had cancer. She didn't feel cute because she had no hair. I guess her mom got tired of when she was saying that so she shaved her hair off. She had times were she bleed out of no where. To get help for her sister could give her kidney. Turns out she didn't want to because she said "what if I need it". Basically she didn't want to risk her life giving her kidney away. Her sister died to.

Down syndrome: a set of mental and physical symptoms and also a chromosomal condition. Down syndrome is also known for trisomy 21. It's named after john Langdon down the British physician who described the syndrome in 1866. It can be identify with amniocentesis during pregnancy.

Chapter4: Teachers

Top three reasons to not let a teacher you don't like interfere with getting your education:

1. A family member (my grandma) might say "what do you not liking the teacher have to do with getting your education."

2. Even though no one in the class like her/him you still have to do your/her work and the principal could come in and tell you "you don't have to like her, but you do need to respect her." That never worked when he told us that.

3. You might have a teacher that can have mood swings, but can be cool sometimes and real. She could

give projects about every month. You could hate her, but still try getting good grades (ME). That's my teacher.

One of my teachers ugh she works my nerves. She's my comm. Arts (communication arts) teacher. NO ONE likes her, but like maybe 10 people. She would ignore us, roll her eyes, and call our parents for reason for no reason. She's like the young, white preppy teachers. She made us shake her hand before we walked in once we all walked in class we got HANDSANTIZIER. Then one day she pushed my friend Paige telling her to get out the class. Turns out she went and wrote and statement and every one that's her teacher want her fired. When we are bad she'd kick us out and say "Idc where you go just get out of my class." On some days she can be *cool, but it DEFINITLY DIDN'T last LONG. I still got a good grade in her class.*

My social studies teacher could be mean, loud and hard on us sometimes, but cool. She let us watch a lot of movies through out the school year. We watched a movie every day in her AE (academic of excellence) class towards the end of the year. Her projects were very organized so that's why it was easy to me. I just didn't like it when she would tell us something then we'd ask her about what she said and would get a whole fit. We just forgot dang chill out.

In elementary all the teachers loved me baby. Who wouldn't?

YOU HAVE TO RESPECT THEM NO MATTER IF YOU DON'T LIKE THEM.

CHAPTER 5: *NO BOYS ALLOWED*

Boys will get you in nothing, but trouble. It's cool for you to have them as your best friends, friend or brother. You don't need to be focusing on them at school, but your education.

I know you want to make money in order to do that you need a good paying job; in order to have that you need an education!!!!!

You don't need to worry about having a boyfriend that's not important. You wanting boys to like you that not important who cares if they don't they can shake!

boys to like you

before | after

hair down
eye shadow
lip gloss, purse
tank top, shirt

pony tail
NO lip gloss
shirt + pants

Even if they call you ugly don't listen to them. Boys will peer pressure you I guaranty you. Worry about them when you're done doing you

When I go to high school (Hazelwood central) I think I want more boy friends. That's because in high school girls start toooo much drama they do the most. Boys would argue or fist fight and be cool the next day. Don't trip on making yourself look good for them to make them like you.

*BYOU BE YOURSELF IN YOUR OWN
WAY!!!!!!!!!!!*

CHAPTER 6: DRAMA

Where to start with drama? Just like who started it? Hmm

RULES FOR WHAT YOU DO AND DON'T DO WHEN WANTING TO FIGHT SOMEONE

1. DON'T TALK BEHIND THEIR BACK THAT'S STARTING MORE STUFF.

2. YOUUUUUUUU SAY EVERYTHINGGGGGG ABOUT THEM TO THEIR FACE

3. DON'T TELL EVERY BODY ABOUT Y'ALL WANTING TO FIGHT (STAFFS, PRINCIPAL DO EAR HUSTLE)

4. DO NOT TEXT OR TALK ON THE PHONE ARUGING

5. DON'T USE PROFANITY!!

6. YOU SHOULD KNOW ABOUT FACEBOOK (A SOCIAL WEBSITE) DON'T RAP ON FACEBOOK

Drama is definitely something you don't want to get into. Drama can get you in big trouble that's why you don't instigate. In middle school that's when drama really starts to go down and get serious. People will talk about you they don't care if they know you or not. You can just walk in the class unn look at her, her ugly self her hair all messed up. It's like is all that really necessary. If you're new don't walk in their school like you run it and you own they school that's going to get you no friends.

When you're in middle school the word fake comes in a lot trust me. Apparently you make a lot of friends and you can be friends with two girls that don't like each other. When they talking about each *other to you and you say "yeah that is right she do be messing with to many boys." Then you talking to the other girl and you say "yeah she is jealous just because you talking to a lot of boys. Also want to talk about that, but that would just be to fake. So when or if that happen to you just be like me I just say "ok" or "well I'm cool with both of yall so just talking about her to me I'm not getting in yall mess." It works every time. Ok now most of the time girls argue or stop talking to each other is because of boys. In 6th grade that's the main reason why them girls was in drama. Don't let a boy ruin your friendship. They also say "how you gone go with my ex" no she can it's natural like for real it's going to happen. I be getting mad when girls be saying that it's like get over it shake brah. They don't say that to me just to let you know.*

In my school we're not allergic to drama why? Well I don't know. Too many girls there start too much sometimes I just want to go off on all of them. We have instigators, rumors, fake people and he said she said. Instigators like to say lies and get into someone else drama (nosey). Kayla was cool with this boy and girl. I'm guessing he told the girl Kayla said this and this about her or whatever. The girl said something about Kayla and guess what? He told Kayla what she said. That's a difference from he said she said because he's telling the truth (I think) about what they saying about each other. I can kind of see why he's doing that maybe because he thinks it right and again this is middle school so NO ITS NOT.

Now it's ridiculous of how many fake people there is.

This other girl would talk all stuff about Kayla for no reason (hater ugh). She would smile in her face and try to be cool again and I think she stopped because Kayla didn't let it get the best of her and didn't give her ……..… . The girl would talk about people, but then when it comes to throwing hands she want to snitch. Whoa sweet baby Jesus mhm.

Rumors is when you can tell your friends and if you didn't just tell one then you wont be able to know who started it. It's not like they gone tell the truth. One of her friends could have told one of her friend then her friend says something else to her friend. I don't think they would do it on purpose. Then basically when they keep telling people it's something different. I'm glad I never had a rumor because it wouldn't be a rumor it would be fighting.

He said she said goes back and forth. Something like no she said "she don't like you" no I didn't I said "sometimes I don't because you start to much stuff" you told me "she don't know how to keep her mouth close because she forever talking about people. I promise you I would go off on both of them like just get over it dang. Girls start too much drama sometimes the boys in it though, but I'm drama free at least I try to be.

If every girl at least every girl was the type that hate being in and starting drama then we would be allergic and my school would be pretty cool. I'm hoping in 8th grade it would be different. Like I said you can also start drama on

Facebook if you have a problem with someone say it to they face. I heard this girl was talking about me my friend told me outside I went to the basketball court and pulled her to the side. We talked settled it because I don't think it was recent so it was nothing and we hugged it out.

There were 6 fights last year. Two in the cafeteria and four in the hallway. I was one in the classroom my class was right next to them. Ok now 6th grade it was 5 of us and this girl would talk about us. Demia (Mia), Tamara (Mara), Trevia (Scooby/Scooby), Brianna (Bre') and me. We would talk all bad about this girl, but she started it. She admitted that she couldn't fight all she did was talk. She thought she was the stuff, but she thought again this year. I spent he night over my ex friends house and the girl that me and my 4 friends would talk about was there sadly. Two or one girl out all stuff on her face I took a picture and now it's on Facebook. I was rollin and she was mad. Guess what? Who cares? We didn't/ don't like her. At my school the hallways are always crowded it seems like something is happening half of the time it is. Just make you stay out and don't start drama and use my rules ☺!

Chapter 7: Career

Whoa a career! I'm far away from having one. I'm only 13! You really don't have to worry about one until high school for real. I do know what I want to be though a…………PEDIATRICIAN!!!!!!!!!!!!!

I love babies/kids. There's one thing I found out a few days ago… I DON'T HAVE TO GIVE THEM SHOTS!!!!! THANK YOU JESUS. I'm terrified of shots. I act like a big baby.

If I can't take it I can't give it you know what I'm saying like for real though.

I also want to be a singer and an actress. I want to be a singer and actress more than being a pediatrician because I've been singing since like 11. I want to be rich so I got to work hard. Being a singer is more of a dream than a career to me. My dad took me to the recorded studio to sing two songs on my b-day. The man that was recording me he said "you put them head phones on like a pro" the second time I did it and I just laughed.

When I'm an actress I want them parts that are funny and fun to do.

When I was 11 and I was watching "house of pain" jasmine "china McClain" I said "I want to have parts just like that." Her parts look easy and fun.

You should want a good career I hope. No matter where you come from or how you are raised shouldn't be an excuse for not wanting a career. You can do anything if you believe and give it your all.

I believe (Yolanda Adams) 1 *believe I can, I believe I will, I believe my hopes and dreams are real. I believe ill stand, I believe ill dance, I believe ill grow real soon and that is why I do believe!!!!!*

That's my song.

Ok now pediatricians earn a lot of money. A lot of people I know want that job because of kids. I look at it as of:

❖ *Saving kids lives*

❖ *Making them healthy*

And

• *Taking them and getting them far in life healthy*

I realized I actually wanted to be a pediatrician, because my bad, but good sometimes baby cousins. My cousin had a boy and girl Taylen and Caitlyn. Of course the girl is the youngest (2). The boy is 4 I think. The weird thing about my cousins is both of them born in October only a few days apart. A secret between us I was mad on the inside when I found out she was having a baby. That's just because I was the youngest out of her, my cousin, my sister and me all girls o yea. When I baby sit them it can fun if they are good like I tell them. What career fits you? Think about it.

Chapter 8: Peer pressure

Of course peer pressure deals with boys. It only deals with hem because they're the ones that peer pressuring me. When you get to a certain well not certain exactly, but that's when you start............ That doesn't just mean pain it means able to get pregnant. As some parents say "I aint raisin no babies." Sex isn't important you can wait. You may think protection will work most the time yes other times no. You may have friends that already had sex that DO NOT mean ANYTHING! You can get aids, hiv or stds.

AIDS: (acquired immune deficiency syndrome)

• Acquired-able to get infected with it.

• Immune deficiency-weakness in the body's system that fights disease.

• Syndrome-a group of health problems that make up a disease

A disease that has a severe loss of the body's cellular immunity. It's caused by a virus hiv. You can "get" aids, just infected with hiv, and then later develop aids. You can get infected with hiv from someone who is infected.

HIV: (human immunodeficiency virus) a retrovirus that causes aids. Get ready to know about HIV. Sit down relax and read.

You CAN NOT get HIV from:

▪ Hugging, shaking or holding hands

▪ Eating off dishes in public places

- *Using the same toilet as someone that has HIV*

- *Getting mosquitoes bites*

- *Breathing air after someone with HIV coughs or sneezes*

- *Living or working with someone that has HIV*

You CAN get HIV from:

❖ *Blood*

❖ *Semen*

❖ *Pre-seminal fluid*

❖ *Vaginal fluid*

❖ *Breast milk*

In order to be transmitted with HIV it must be presented in one person to be transmitted to another. HIV must enter into the blood stream of the other person.

It can enter the blood stream through these sites on the human body:

o *Vein*

o *Under the skin*

o *In the muscle*

o *"skin popping"*

o *Butt*

o *Vagina*

o *Urethra*

o *Mouth*

o *Cuts or sores*

THAT'S PROBABLY WHY YOU WEAR BAND-AIDS

The main ways HIV is transmitted is:

o *Sharing needles*

o Sexual contact

o Vaginal

o Anal (butt)

o Oral

Just by learning about HIV I don't even want a baby when I'm old. So think again when a boy tries to peer pressure you. Having sex isn't just simple or not a big idea. Having sex comes with a lot of CONSEQUNCES!

STDS: (sexually transmitted disease) also known as STI (sexually transmitted infection) and VD (venereal disease). It's an illness that has significant probability of transmission between humans. By means of human sexual behavior. STD is the same thing as HUV.

I HOPE BY READING THAT IT MAKES YOU WANT TO THINK TWICE

BEFORE YOU HAVE SEX ESPECIALLY AT A YOUNG AGE.

(ALL INFORMATION AND INFORMATION IN OTHER CHAPTERS FROM GOOGLE.)

CHAPTER 9: ALL ABOUT ME

MY name is Aria Monique Bryant I love my mommy, daddy, sister, grandma and family.

I love my friends Jayla, Kayla, Shandon, Devyn, Trevia, A.J, Cimoia, Justin, Kayla T, Lauren, Bryce, TANASHA, Josh, Lavoid, Paige, Kayla M, Kamia, Chaz, Charles, Christian, Corlanda, Samesha, Ayanna, Aliyah, Kkelsie, DAMAREA, Deshayla, Karissa, Alayah, Andrew, Jordan W, Elaine, ASHLEY, Rachel, Mikey, and Tweety.

I was born on March10, 1998 in northwest Christian hospital.

As you know I'm 13 and I go to Hazelwood north middle school and in 7th grade going to 8th.

I'm in band play the flute (1st chair) and I'm in girl scouts.

I'm a cheerleader, gymnast, dancer, singer, actress, flute player, fashion designer and song writer.

I do volleyball, hair and nails.

I like playing on my ipod, talking on the phone, texting, listening to music, singing songs, eating, hanging with friends, swimming, bowling, going outside, skating, going to the movies, shopping, miniature gulfing, playing the wii, go to my friends house, doing friendship bracelets and collecting quarters.

My favorite artist is:

❖ TREY SONGZ	❖ NEYO
❖ USHER	❖ MICHEAL JACKSON
❖ CHRIS BROWN	❖ KIRK FRANKLIN
❖ DRAKE	❖ MARVIN SAPP
❖ NICKI MINAJI	❖ TYE TRIBETT
❖ KE$HA	❖ DONALD LAWRENCE
❖ MINDLESS BEHAVIOR	❖ BOW WOW
❖ TRAVIS POTER	❖ TIFFANY EVENS

❖ ROSCOE DASH	❖ T.I
❖ LIL WAYNE	❖ KESHIA COLE
❖ LIL TWIST	❖ PLEASURE P
❖ Waka flaka	❖ MARCUS OPPER
❖ WIZ KHALIFA	❖ JADEN
❖ KHALIL	❖ WILLOW
❖ KERI HILSON	❖ Jasmine Sullivan
❖ JACOB LATIMORE	❖ LISA TUCKER
❖ DIGGY	❖ SOULJA BOY
❖ ALOHA	❖ NEW BOYZ
❖ Justin	❖ OMG GIRLZ

Bieber	
❖ BEYONCE'	❖ MONICA
❖ ALICIA KEYS	❖ CYMPHONI-QUE
❖ FANTASIA	❖ NEYO
❖ AUBURN	❖ MICHEAL JACKSON

That was a lot!

!At my school I have a friend named Bryce he can be funny sometimes. He is super cool. We have 3 things in common

- basketball

- In band (he play sax.)

- The team Dallas

My favorite 2 songs right now are next 2 you and butterflies!

"I cant help but smile when I see you my heart beats so fast when I'm around you I cant control what I feel inside (you give me butterflies) put me on cloud nine. You're the one who really understands me I can be who I am you never try to change me. Even when it rains and I'm going through things you're always there and you never complain.

CYMPHONIQUE

Here are the names of my songs:

❖ *You'll change into an angel*

❖ *We ready*

❖ *Its me*

❖ *No script*

- ❖ *Teenage love*
- ❖ *Party party*
- ❖ *Baby boo*
- ❖ *Waste no time*
- ❖ *Ill be there*
- ❖ *Byou (recently new)*

I love my friends and we have insiders:

Me and Kayla

- *I like fresh crayons out the pack*
- *Squishy booty*
- *You cant resist my eyes*
- *Really*
- *We in there like swim wear*

Me and Shandon

- *Where my cookies at?*

- *I see you*

Me and A.J

- *Your not the boom.com*

- *Im sick of this*

- *Your not hot*

- *You fruit loop*

- *I don't know nothing 'bout nothing*

- *Salute*

- *Toddles*

It be hilarious l2h

I have 6 favorite sayings:

❖ *Shut don't go up crises do so take your advice and shut up to.*

❖ *I don't shut up I grow up every time I see yo face I throw up*

❖ *Honk if you love Jesus text while driving if you want to me him*

❖ *Sweet baby Jesus*

❖ *Guess what? Chicken butt put it in a cup go around and lick it up*

❖ *Snaps and claps for arie*

Shandon's is:

- *That jimmy boy*

- *Cheez-it*

- *Yeaa*

Me and my friend Chris we have a song that we should sing "what the heck" Avril Lavigne. One of us would sing it and if I hear him I would come in.

Ok I'm also in this black history play it's called "risen." Were going to Atlanta, Washington, and were doing it here in Saint Louis too. My play director told me were going to Atlanta just me and his son to do a casting call. We special because we get to do it private unlike every one else. He only told me that the director is Kyle and Christopher dad. I'm so happy I can't wait to go.

When I txt I like to do these:

:) :(:[:] ;) :'(T.T O_O O.O :O <3 :P :-D >:(:-> XD

You already know that I like designing and I draw clothes. I have a whole binder for designing. When I grow up I'm getting my own fashion line. You have to be positive in yourself and say your getting it. My is *line is going to be called "ARA-BEAU." I got the ara from my name just not with the "I." Beau comes beautiful. Famous people rappers and singers do. Lil wayne and cymphonique did.*

I loves my grandma she super cool. I act like a baby when I spend the night with her. I would ask her to make me some dinner. In 6th grade reading class we had to write about who's our hero. I guess you know it's my grandma and I said…..

My hero is my grandma. She is really nice. The vibe of her house just makes me happy and so does she. She is also an independent and Christian woman. Ever since we moved into our new house shed helped us. My grandma is helpful and I say that because every first Monday

of every month I want to do praise
and worship at my church. She
comes from Illinois to Missouri to get
me when I get off my bus just for that.
She's really my hero. She gave my
grandma some money for school
supplies. My grandma crochets and
sew I learned both of them.
Sometimes I would go in her room,
sit on her bed, and crochet with her. I
love spending quality time with my
grandma. One day I might go outside
and do her yard work.

She encourages me so much.
Some of my family members say I
like to entertain people and I'm muti
talented. Sometimes I would dance
or sing for her when I was little before
I go to bed.

Our tradition is she cooks after church everyyyyyyyyyy Sunday unless our church having dinner.

My grandma makes the most incredible apple pie. When I eat it it feels like I'm in heaven. I can eat the whole pie. I pray for her every night and when I'm with her I try to make sure she's safe. I want her to stay forever and ever. I love her so much. I'm a grandma's granddaughter.

I remember when I was like ten maybe nine me and my friends would just be like I want to name my daughter or son this when I grow up. Haven't you done that with your friends? Now I'm 13 so I know now.

Girls oldest-youngest

- *Cymphonique Ariya Bryant*
- *Marcia Marie Bryant*
- *Erin Uniqe Bryant*
- *Harmony Joy Bryant*
- *Sha'Rae Diamond Bryant*
- *Miyah Nae Bryant*
- *Kaziah Devyn Bryant*
- *Layla Dania Bryant*

Boys oldest-youngest

- *Andre' dametrious Bryant*
- *Prodajy Saxon Bryant*
- *Trey Aireis Bryant*
- *Drake Quentez Bryant*

❖ *Justin La'Ron Bryant*

Im not having all of them I just like those names. You already know I got trey fro trey songz and drake from drake and prodajy from mindless behavior.

Yall know I know I love Kayla and also my other 2 friend's jayla and tanasha. Jayla is like my booski, my older sister for life. Tanasha is my wifey and by wifey my best friend out of every one. I love her to death.

It was a serious storm at school while we were at lunch. We sit in the back where it's all windows. It looked like a tornado was about to drop people were screaming and the lights off. She started crying and I held her and she sits next to me. I was trying to make her stop and I was telling her everything is going to be ok. She was only crying because she knew her mom was out there driving. To be honest I didn't care about nobody else but her. I couldn't walk with her upstairs to class because we didn't have the same class. I made sure someone walked up there with her.

KAYLA V. JORDAN

JAYLA COLLINS

TANASHA DAVIS

KOOL

AWSOME

YELLS

LAZY

ANNOYING LOL

JOYFUL

OUTRAGES

REAL

DEPENDABLE

A LEADER

NICE (SOMETIMES)

JOYFUL

AWSOME

YELLS

LAZY

ANGEL

CARING

OUTRAGES

LOVING

LOVE ABLE

INTELLIGENT

NICE

SILLY

TRUSTWORTHY

ANGRY

NICE

ANGEL

SILLY

HYPER

AWSOME

DEPENDABLE

A GOOD FRIEND

VERY RELIABLE

IRREPALCEABLE

SINCERE

I have been talking about yall getting your education so I'm going to tell you my past grades. Yes it's all true because I have a book where I can put my grades and school memories in.

Kindergarten-   I mostly had "I" (independent): the student understands and uses the skill constantly.

1st grade-mostly "d" (developing): understands and uses the skill some of the time.

2nd grade-mostly "NA" (not assessed at this time)

3rd grade-comm. Arts final grade b-82% math b-87% science b-82%

health b-82% gym a-93% art a-100% music a-95% social studies b from an a-92% omg b-89%

4th grade-comm. Arts c-81% math b-88% science a-93% s.s. b-87% health a-96% gym a-92% art a-95% music a-98% band (flute) a-94%

5th grade-comm. Arts b-86% math a-94% science a-97% s.s. b-91% health a-95% gym a-94% art a-96% band a-98%

6th grade-comm. Arts a-100% math a-92% science a-97% s.s. a-96% NO HEALTH gym a-94% NO ART band b-90%

Pretty good huh?

HOW TO STAY FRESH

❖ *All the work your body is doing you need to bathe or shower daily especially if your active*

❖ *No girl can look or feel good with drugs in her body. They can mess up your future and family. If your smart you would walk away from so called friends that tell you its not bad just try it.*

❖ *Do keep it clean*

❖ *Do dechlorinate*

❖ *Wash your comb and brush*

❖ *Don't over heat*

❖ *Don't share*

❖ *Do manage*

- *With braces brush after every meal and floss*

- *Brush teeth regularly*

- *Bathe or shower regularly*

- *Take care of your hair*

- *Drink sprite, sierra mist or 7up when you have cramps and lay down*

- *Take care of your nails*

- *Wash your face*

- *Drink water*

- *Eat breakfast to start your day off right*

- *Don't eat junk food a lot*

- *Go outside for at least an hr everyday for exercise*

ONE FASHION TIP

o *Try to keep up with the latest thing like how when Nike flip flops came out or Griffey's (shoes). Do keep in mind to try to do you. Like when Nike flip flops came out I got them but mike was in PINK instead.*

Key

AJ- AJ invented

SB-Shandon invented

Ken.- Kenny invented

Sayings

- o *Best believe*

- o *Get out here wit all dat*

- o *Mmkay*

- o *Boy please*

- *Dismissed sweetheart*
- *Who you talkin to*
- *No sweetie*
- *Honey boo boo*
- *Dismissed!*
- *Sweet heart*
- *Sweetie pie*
- *Wifey*
- *BYOU*
- *I'm my own me in my own way*
- *Believe it or leave*
- *Toddles-AJ*
- *Your not hot-AJ*
- *I'm sick of this-AJ*

- *Your not the boom.com-AJ*
- *Fruit loop-AJ*
- *Shut it down-AJ*
- *Get off my phone/line-AJ*
- *I don't know nothing bou nothing-AJ*
- *Cheez-it-SB*
- *That jimmy boy-SB*
- *Yeaa (the way he say it)-SB*
- *Are you serious?*
- *Calm down*
- *Chill out*
- *Heyy boo*
- *Wow*
- *O kkkk*

- *Thank ummz*
- **cough cough**
- *Cough you*
- *You read me (when texting)*
- *You hear me*
- *You feel me*
- *No stuff*
- *No dice*
- *Sike*
- *Sure ok*
- *That's what you say*
- *That's how you feel now*
- *That's how we doing it*
- *Is you mad*
- *Don't be actin brand new*

- *I see you*
- *What you on*
- *Brah*
- *You hipp*
- *Haha/hehe*
- *Im hollin*
- *Booski*
- *Where they do dat at*
- *Right*
- *You needs to stops*
- *Lolxz*
- *Smh*
- *G2g*
- *Live, laugh, love*
- *Btw*

- *Boo*
- *You do the most*
- *Tell me why*
- *Jk, jp*
- *Tbt- truth be told*
- *Shameful*
- *You to extra*
- *L2h*
- *Lmbo*
- *Idk, idc*
- *Heck naw*
- *Im to mad*
- *Hilarious*
- *Girl boo*
- *Im rollin*

- *Shake*

- *Really*

- *We in there like swim wear*

- *We in there*

- *Get off me (the way he say it)-AJ*

- *Bust a move*

- *Do something*

- *Not at all*

- *Oh no-ken*

- *Ttly*

- *Hit me up lata*

- *You hurt*

- *That's on you*

- *Salute-AJ*

For more information, advice, or just wanting to talk e-mail me at: ariabryant159cupcake@yahoo.com

If you have a facebook add me Aria Bryant

Thank umzzzz

NOW SOMETHING FOR YOU TO DO

MY GOOD, FUN, HAPPY, DAYS

Date: _____

_____

_____

_____

_____

Date: _____

_____

_____

_____

_____

Date: _____

_____

_____

_____

_____

Date: _____

_____

_____

_____

_____

Date: _____

_____

_____

_____

_____

Date: _____

_____

_____

_____

_____

Drama day

Date: _____

_____

_____

_____

_____

Date: _____

_____

_____

_____

_____

Date: _____

_____

_____

_____

_____

Date: _____

_____

_____

_____

_____

Date: _____

_____

_____

_____

_____

Date: _____

_____

_____

_____

_____

Date: _____

_____

_____

_____

_____

My sad days

Date: _____

_____
_____
_____

Date: _____

_____
_____
_____

_____

Date: _____

_____
_____
_____

_____

Date: _____

_____
_____
_____

_____

_____

Date: _____

_____

_____

_____

_____

I was so heated

Date: _____

_____

_____

_____

_____

Date: _____

_____

_____

_____

_____

Date: _____

_____

_____

_____

_____

Date: _____

_____

_____

_____

_____

Date: _____

_____

_____

_____

_____

Date: _____

_____

_____

_____

Date: _____

Jealous day

Date: _____

Date: _____

Date: _____

Date: _____

Date: _____

Date: _____

Date: _____

I'm so in love today

Date: _____

_____
_____
_____

_____

Date: _____

_____
_____
_____

Date: _____

_____
_____
_____

Date: _____

_____
_____
_____
_____

Date: _____

_____

_____

_____

_____

Date: _____

_____

_____

_____

_____

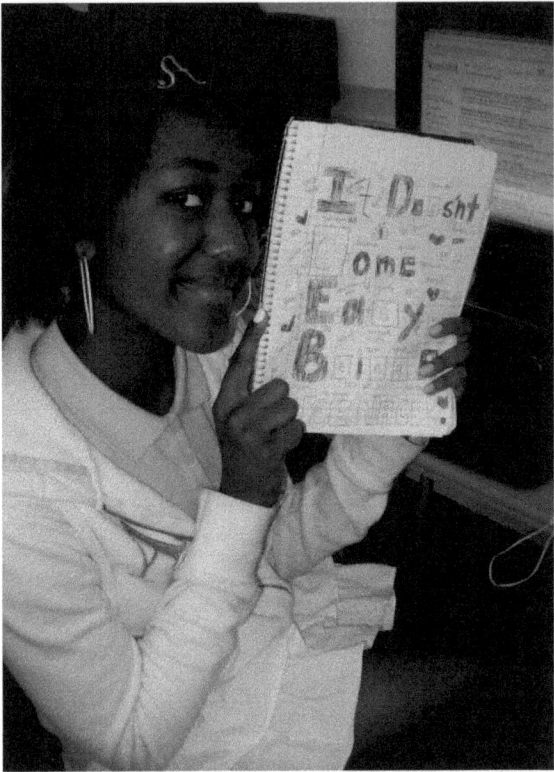

The beginning stages of writing my book.

After writing my story, it was time to type it.

Ms. Owens and Ms. Robinson helping me
during the camp.

Reading my typed manuscript.

Listening to a guest speaker during the camp.

The campers at City Hall being recognized
for becoming Jr. Authors.

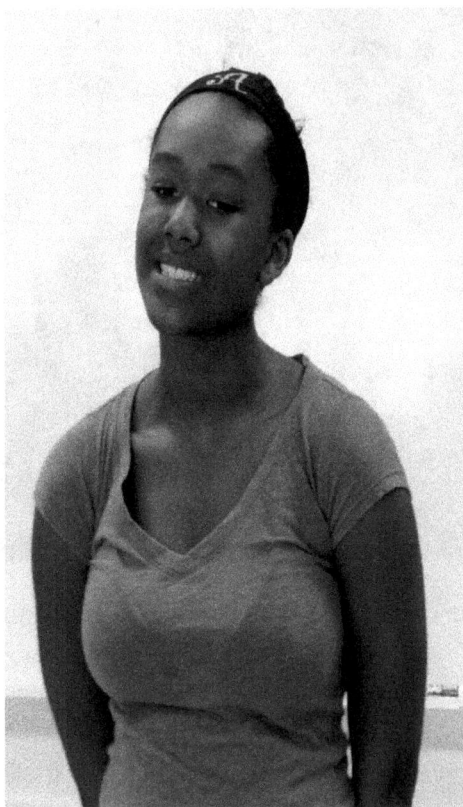

Standing in front of the class for a class activity.

About The Risen Foundation

The RISEN Foundation is a Missouri non-profit corporation. Our ultimate goal is to empower school age kids through the arts by creating innovative educational tools, and entertaining programs that will build their confidence, future and career path.

Overall, our programs are created to empower today youth in order for them to gain the necessary building skills, tools and accomplishments to add onto their college portfolio and future job resumes. Each student will walk away with a great sense of pride and increased self-confidence.

Our Programs:

"Publishing Camp 4 Kids" - is designed to turn your child into a published author while promoting literacy and increasing their interest in the art of reading and writing.

"RISE to Education International Book & School Supply Drive" - is another program where we give back! We has identified various schools in developing countries that are lacking some of the bare essentials that we believe every child deserves; educational supplies.

"Jr. Internship Program" – is "Inspiration Delivered" and is offered to students starting at 2nd grade level. Students will be given the opportunity to learn from selected professions and volunteer and train under their business professional in the following career paths: Law, Medicine, Politics, Medicine, Science, and Technology.

"*Interactive Educational Theater*" - program focuses on writing and producing educational stage plays in which students are given the opportunity to participate in the production in various capacities. The program is geared to giving school age children a chance at theater and what it is all about.

Current Productions:

"RISEN: the Stage Play"

For More Information please visit us at www.therisenfoundation.org or email us at info@therisenfoundation.org.

Anthony M. McDonald, Sr.,

Founder & Executive Director

About the Sponsor – The Engine 9 Experience

The Engine 9 Experience Inc., is a St. Louis based video production company founded in 2007by filmmaker Aziza Harris with only a small handheld camcorder, no tripod and little knowledge that she would soon fall in love with the craft of videography.

The Engine 9 Experience, Inc. concentrates its efforts on helping people tell their stories and share their messages with those who might otherwise never hear their voices. Our desire to stay true to the heart and soul of our clients projects has helped us to become a sought after videography company for personal documentaries, video press kits and live event video production.

The Engine 9 Experience, Inc.'s founder & CEO Ms. Harris has a passion for teaching her craft to all who are interested in her field but especially school age children. The Engine 9 Experience inducted an intern program which now has several members who assist her with projects throughout the year.

For more information about The Engine 9 Experience, feel free to visit their website at: www.theengine9experience.com.

About the Sponsor – Nia'fidahli

Nia'fidahli (pronounced NEE-AH-FEE-DAH-LEE) is a small grassroots organization co-founded by two sisters, Aja La'Starr and Adrienne Draper and their high school classmate Mario Gardner. Nia'fidahli is a Kiswahili word meaning "progress," and its primary mission is to utilize diverse initiatives to promote awareness about issues that affect the African American community. Nia'fidahli started off as a bi-weekly, internationally recognized newsletter publication and has evolved into a fundraising organization. Over the years, Nia'fidahli has brought together educators, visual artists, and musicians in the community to raise money for selected disadvantaged groups such as the homeless and people affected by natural disasters. Nia'fidahli prides itself on changing communities through collectively collaborating with other small companies and non-profit organizations to meet all of their goals-locally as well as abroad.

For more information about Nia'fidahli, feel free to visit their website at: www.niafidahli.com.

About the Sponsor – RSRG Attorneys at Law

ROSENBLUM, SCHWARTZ, ROGERS & GLASS, P.C. is a nationally recognized criminal defense firm dedicated to defending individuals and corporations facing all levels of state and federal investigations and prosecutions. The firm has long been regarded as one of the premier criminal defense firms based upon successful results in the most difficult and complex matters.

The firm brings more than 130 years of combined expert legal experience in the field of criminal defense and white collar crimes. We provide each client with legal excellence, aggressive representation, honesty, integrity and extraordinary client services. The firm utilizes the collective skills and experiences of each of our attorneys to provide the maximum benefit to each and every client.

For more information about RSRG at Law, feel free to visit their website at: www.rsrglaw.com. Attorney Joel Schwartz 314-862-4332.

About the Sponsor – Impact St. Louis

IMPACT St. Louis was created to provide innovative and educational youth development programs and activities to children who have limited access to community and social service programs. Through our partnerships with schools and community- based organizations, we are able to create a lasting impact in the lives of our youth, their families and ultimately the St. Louis community.

IMPACT has been serving the youth of St. Louis since 2008. Alderman Greg Carter, of the 27th ward, saw the need for additional resources for kids in his neighborhood and worked with the St. Louis Mental Health Board and The 100 Black Men of Metro St. Louis to start a program that provided holistic programs for youth. In the first two years, IMPACT partnered with 25 different organizations and served over 400 kids in the St. Louis area in the areas of gang and crime prevention, drug and substance abuse prevention, mentoring, health and fitness, tutoring and literacy.

For more information about Impact St. Louis, feel free to visit their website at: www.impactstl.org.

About the Sponsor – 100 Black Men of Metropolitan St. Louis

The overall concept of the 100 began in New York in 1963 when a group of concerned African American men began to meet to explore ways of improving conditions in their community. The group eventually adopted the name, "100 Black Men, Inc." as a sign of solidarity. These men envisioned an organization that would implement programs designed to improve the quality of life for African Americans and other minorities.

They also wished to ensure the future of their communities by aiming an intense number of resources toward youth development. These members were successful black men from various walks of life.

Mission:

To improve the quality of life enhance educational and economic opportunities in our community.

For more information about 100 Black Men of Metropolitan St. Louis, feel free to visit their website at: www.100blackmenstl.org.

www.ingramcontent.com/pod-product-compliance
Lightning Source LLC
Chambersburg PA
CBHW071639050426
42443CB00026B/735